CONTENTS

WHAT WILL MAKE
HIM LEAVE

For Good

Elizabeth A. James

INTRODUCTION

Hi, my name is Elizabeth and my friends call me *"Rose."* Let me tell you a little about myself first. I own an advice column where I give advice to people daily. Over the past fifteen plus years, I've helped thousands of others just like you. Most of the questions I get have to do with their relationship. So, chances are any questions you have, I've already helped someone else with the same problem. I give advice on a few different websites online for free, trying to help as many people, couples, and families as I can. I didn't really do my advice online until covid-19 came along, but just like others I had to change things up a little. The name of my advice column is *"Love Talk 911,"* you can find it on a few different social media accounts. I'm just now getting a little better at the new way of doing things. I was trying to figure out a way that I could be able to reach more people just like you and I. So, I thought one way I could do that is to write a book. However, I can only cover a few things at a time in my books. Hoping that if someone is facing a relationship problem, or has a question you might find it in one of my books. Not only that it's not going to cost you hundreds or thousands of dollars. This book you are going to learn things that will drive your man away for good. A lot of ladies have asked me this very question. So, I did a survey on over five hundred men to get to the closest answer I could. So, if you feel like he is pulling away from you, it might be because of something in this book. Maybe, after reading your relationship can start back fresh again. I hope you enjoy and find the answers you're looking for.

HE IS AFRAID OF HIS FEELING

You might be thinking "afraid of his feelings." But yes, that is what I mean and what I am saying. After talking to so many different men over the years and asking them why they leave their relationship. A high percent of them said it was because of how they started feeling, and it scared them. It wasn't because of another girl/woman, it wasn't because they weren't happy, it was because of being afraid of how they were feeling.

They may be feeling the same way you are, the only thing is they don't know how to express their feelings back to you. When they are at this point it causes a lot of worry in them that they aren't keeping you happy, or worry that you don't think they really care when they do. A lot of men I have come across have this ego thing that keeps them from showing emotions, or allowing them to be emotional. Now, not every man has that ego problem to where they can't express how they feel. However, the ones that do, when they start to feel these emotions it can be overwhelming and cause them to leave the relationship so they don't have to feel that way.

He could also be afraid that it is a disappointment or that he is disappointing you by not showing or saying how he feels. All men know that women like to be told and shown that we are cared for and wanted. So do men, the problem is if they can't express that to us, they may feel they are letting us down. That fear can make them leave the relationship for good.

If you think your partner/husband/boyfriend is having this problem, a problem with expressing his/themself talk to them about it. Let them know, you know how they feel and that it's okay to not express all your feelings at once.

BEING PRESSURED

We all like to make our own decisions in what we do and when we do it. Men take great pride in this area of their life. Back to that ego thing, so many men don't like to think they have to answer to no one. Or think they have to be told what to do, they look at this as being pressured.

If he starts feeling like he is being pressured into doing something, chances are he will walk. Men don't like the feeling of being pushed into nothing. So, pushing them over and over about when you're going to start a family, have kids, get pets, move in together etc.. can push him over the edge to where they leave the relationship.

He may also feel pressure from his friends or coworkers. If his friends/coworkers are nagging him about the relationship or you, it could cause him to pull away so they stop. Think of it this way; if he does have feelings for you, and he's hanging out less with his friends, or stops altogether. They may call him "chicken picked, say he is whipped, etc.." Being called or nagged can put a lot of pressure on anyone. He may be happy with you and in the relationship, but the pressure from others could make him pull away or leave to show he isn't what they are calling him.

If you start to think that this could be a problem in your relationship, or if you hear his friends/coworkers or even family nag or crack jokes at him; maybe it would be a good idea to sit down and talk to him about it. Ask him how he is feeling about what is being said. Ask him if he feels like you are pressuring him, this way if you're not aware of it, then you can work on it.

Think of it if it was you. How would you feel if you felt pressured into doing something, acting someway, or being nagged by your family, friends, or coworkers. What would you do? Would you talk to him, or pull away just hoping it would all stop?

YOUR GOING TO LEAVE THEM

Sometimes men get it in their head that you're going to leave them. This can be due to a lot of different reasons. Some of the ones I was told were; "I made her mad and I thought she was going to leave me, so I left." "The relationship was having problems, and I thought she started liking someone else, so I left." "A friend said they saw her with someone else at what time I was gone, so I left."

Each reason has to do with someone telling them something or someone joking and it ends up causing them to walk out of your life and the relationship for good.

I have had a few cases where the men were dating the girls and said they had been together a long time and they thought it was going to end, so they left the relationship first.

If you have or think that this could be the problem in your relationship, just talk to your husband, partner, boyfriend. Talking to them could fix a misunderstanding and keep your relationship together.

WORK STRESS

Oh, the stress of work! What it can do to you and your relationship. This is one of the top reasons why men and women walk away from a relationship for good. However, this book is based on why men walk away.

When men get stressed out they don't know how to express their feelings, and sometimes they come off as being a dick. Everyone reacts differently when it comes to stress, and how they deal with it. If he is stressed and you are overthinking everything, that could push him to pull away and leave the relationship.

If he starts feeling overwhelmed and doesn't understand why, he may think leaving would be the thing that could fix it. Another thing, sometimes stress from work can cause partners to argue. If he is having to stay longer or later, and you just want to spend time with him; but he knows you both need the money. That can lead to tension, which then leads to arguing. The arguing leads to him walking out the door. He does this because to him you do not understand what he is trying to do for the both of you.

If this seems like it could be the problem in your relationship right now just talk to others. Come up with a way where you both can still have time for each other, and still know what has to be done.

Try to remember that stress works on everyone differently, and the only way any relationship can get through a stressful time is to talk, talk, talk.

THE LOVE & ATTRACTION IS FADING OR GONE.

We all know when it's good it's good. However, we should also understand that sometimes love & attractions can fade away. That isn't any one person's fault, it just happens sometimes in relationships.

This can happen right out of the blue. However, it has been building up over time. Most times when men are in a relationship for a long period of time and everything feels like it's the same they can tend to lose interest. When they start to lose interest they will pull away.

They will pull away in different forms/ways. If your men don't want to have sex, or just don't touch/kiss you anymore; chances are they have lost love & attraction for you. You can also tell if he is pulling away because of this, he will physically try staying away from you. He isn't doing this to hurt you, but sometimes they don't know how to express that is what it is.

Once it's gotten to a point they will just walk out of the relationship without saying a word. They will just leave and not come back. However, there are a few that will try to start an argument so they have a reason to leave.

If you think this is a problem that your relationship is headed towards, work on it NOW. If you and your partner have been together for a long period of time, and things in your sex life have slowed down, my advice is to do something to bring the spice back. Because when he gets to that last point nothing will stop him from leaving.

JEALOUSY

This is a well-known reason why men walk away from their partners, girlfriends, wifes. Jealousy can come in different forms and ways as well. We all know how things can get stuck in our head because something we saw, was told, or even just thought about. That is where jealousy comes from and it is the cause of a lot of relationships ending.

If he starts to think that there is something going on with you and someone else, he will walk away. Men don't know how to control their emotions so they most of the time do one of two things. Get really mad or walk away from it all.

If he sees you acting friendly "in his mind" then you are doing something with that person. This stems back to the fear of you leaving him, and his scared feelings. This could cause him to leave thinking you're going to leave him for that person.

Okay, that covers a couple reasons why he would maybe get jealous and walk away. But you need to keep in mind that he will want to leave you if you're too jealous. When men like their freedom, if they aren't doing anything and it all in your head. Then he most likely will walk away, because you're not listening to him. Instead, you're overreacting because of how you are feeling.

To some this one up, men can get stuck in their head just like anyone else. If they start thinking you're seeing someone else, or if you start being too jealous chances are they will want to leave the relationship.

If you know this is where your relationship is heading, or you are already in this situation with your boyfriend, husband, and/or partner the best thing you could do is try to fix and change the situation; now that's if you still want to be in the relationship. Sometimes, when someone starts getting jealous it can be too much for someone to deal with. Always think about your health and happiness. Try to remember that jealousy comes in many different shapes, forms, and ways.

MOTHERING THEM

I've seen this happen so many times in different relationships. When we love someone we want to take care of them, we want them to know we will do anything for them. This is fine however, it can lead to overly "mothering them."

Most couples I've talked to will say they love & enjoy when their partner does something for them. This can be if you cook for them, clean, wash their clothing, wake them up for work, even take showers with them, and wash them off. These are all okay if that is what you both enjoy. However, this can lead to you treating them like a child, or them feeling you're treating them like a child. Has your partner, boyfriend, husband ever looked at you and said "You're not my mother!" If so, that is because you are taking care of them too far.

The more you care for them and tend to their needs, other behaviors start to creep in. You will think you can tell them when they need to be home, or where they can and can not go. Men don't like being told what they can and can not do. If they normally have poker night with their buddies and you tell them they don't need to go; to them you are trying to be their mother. This will not work in any relationship. If you tell them they need to slow down drinking or not to drink at a party, they look at it as if you're telling them what to do. I can understand worrying about the person you love and care for, however, don't take things over board.

Now, if you see something that they are doing that is going to hurt them, yes, tell them about it, but don't act like their mother and tell them what they have to do. Try talking to them. If you are in this situation in your relationship and didn't even know it, talk to them. We tend to get here and don't know when or how it all started. However, if things don't change quickly, they will walk out of the relationship for good.

HE STILL CARES FOR HIS EX

This is one we hope isn't the reason for him leaving especially if we still care and love them. However, men fall hard when they fall in love. Their emotions and how they react to them are different from women, and different from others.

When they care for someone their feelings just don't go away after the relationship ends. So, if they bump into one of their ex's and their feelings come rushing back, that could cause them to pull away and walk out until they figure things out.

If they start pulling away and everything in the relationship is good and you can't think what could be going on, there's a good chance it could be this. Try talking to them and hoping they will tell you. If they start making things up that don't really make sense to you, most likely it's an ex's or someone new.

If this is the problem in your relationship maybe it's time to move on yourself. You don't want or need to be in a relationship with someone that can't put you first in their life. You want to have all their love and attention, not just what they can give you at the time.

YOU BOTH WANT DIFFERENT PATHS

This is a hard one not just for you but them as well. We can love and care for someone so much, however, we still want to follow our dreams.

If he is looking to the future with you, but he sees that his and your path is heading somewhere different it could cause him to leave the relationship. Not because he doesn't love you, in fact he loves you so much that he still wants you to follow your dreams.

For example, say you both have a dream job and at the time you two got together that dream job was still a ways off. However, now you're in reach of your dream and he's a little behind you. Your dream leads you to a different city, but he has to stay for his work, so his dream will come. He could end the relationship so you can follow your dreams. Or the other way around if he leaves and you are staying.

If this is the situation your relationship is in right now, talk to each other and try working things out, that's if you want to stay in the relationship. I know a lot of relationships don't like to think about long-distance relationships, but that might be a starting point to see if your relationship can work in the long run.

CAN'T SEE EYE TO EYE

Even when we love someone, sometimes it is hard to see eye to eye on some things. Like I've said a few times everyone feels and reacts differently to different situations. He could feel like the only thing left to do is leave the relationship.

If you and him are fighting and arguing over different things, he may start to think that you can't see eye to eye on nothing. Before some will sit around and fight and argue all the time they will just leave.

If your relationship is more fighting and arguing over everything that could make him leave for good. At a point in anyone's life if something makes them unhappy more than happy they are left thinking "what is the use of it?"

If this is the problem or you can see this is the way things are headed for your relationship, my advice is talk to him about it before it gets to that point. If it's already at that point it's just left to when will he leave or you.

THE WEDGE

The wedge can be the cause of a lot of things. One of the biggest I've come across while helping others was hidden feelings and tendson for other problems in the relationship.

This one can go long with not seeing eye to eye. Say your relationship was headed toward fighting and arguing all the time, and over every little thing. You both talk about the situation and things start to get better. However, he didn't tell you how he really felt, and kept his thoughts to himself. He just wanted things to stop and go back to normal. With doing that it puts a wedge between you two and the relationship. After a while passes and the problem is not really fixed, it builds up tension. Which leads him to feeling he wasn't heard, and pulls away from you. Then you start feeling him pull away, and it causes him to leave the relationship. That is only one way a wedge can get into your relationship.

Another one, is if someone said something to him about you, example: (they saw you talking to your ex). If he doesn't know how to express his feelings and thoughts about what was said, it can cause tension and a wedge in your relationship. Instead of talking about it, he lets his thoughts get the best of him. He then is left feeling the only thing left to do is leave the relationship for good.

If you think a wedge might be in your relationship, find it fast. Wedges are known to cause a lot of broke-ups and divorces.

CONCLUSION

Relationships can start off strong and be good for a long time. However, if we don't watch and work on our relationship it is sure to end. No relationship runs on autopilot. We have to work at it if we want it to last. All relationships will have their ups and downs. All couples will have their fights and arguments. We all have a past, and all this is normal, we are humans. It's how we handle each problem and situation in our relationships.

When you start to notice that something isn't right don't just overlook it, not even the small problems; they can lead to bigger ones that can't be fixed. Talk to each other daily and let each other know how your day went. If your partner, husband, boyfriend makes you upset, let them know. Tell them to do the same thing. This will help you from placing that unwanted wedge. Let them know you care for them, but don't over do it and try being their mother. Don't push him into nothing, give him the time he needs, after all you wouldn't want pushed into something you are not ready for. Last, give him a little space. It's okay if you two aren't together 24/7.

I hope you learn something from reading this book. I hope that if you are finding yourself in one of the situations or problems above you know what to do. I wish all of you the happiest and best relationship. Love each other and show it in what you do and say. Good luck in the years to come.

More Information

You can find more information about who I am and how long I have been helping relationships by just a simple google search. My name is Elizabeth but friends call me Rose. If you find yourself needing help and/or advice on something in your relationship you can search for Love Talk 911 or you can email me at my personal email lovetalk911.advicecolumn@gmail.com.

I wish you the best of luck in your relationship for years to come. I hope you get what you're looking for and what you need in life. Remember, Look out for them "Red Flags" when starting a new relationship.